JESUS IS ALIVE

THE AMAZING STORY

TOLD BY CARINE MACKENZI
ILLUSTRATIONS BY FRED AP

Copyright © 1998 Carine Mackenzie
ISBN: 978-1-85792-344-5
Reprinted 2001, 2004, 2007, 2009, 2012 and 2017
Published by Christian Focus Publications, Geanies House,
Fearn, Tain, Ross-shire, IV20 1TW, Scotland, U.K.
www.christianfocus.com
Printed in China

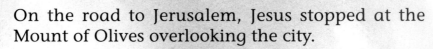

On the road to Jerusalem, Jesus stopped at the Mount of Olives overlooking the city.

'Go to that village over there,' he told two of his disciples. 'You will find a young donkey. Bring it to me.'

The disciples brought the young donkey, and put some of their clothes on its back. Jesus rode into Jerusalem. Crowds of people joined the procession.

Some cut down branches from the palm trees and placed them on the ground in front of Jesus. Others laid down their cloaks.

The crowd shouted out joyfully, 'Hosanna to the Son of David. Blessed is he that comes in the name of the Lord.'

Jesus rode right into the town.

It was time for the Passover Feast. Jesus sent two of his disciples ahead to get ready for it.

'Follow the man you will meet who will be carrying a jar of water,' said Jesus. 'He will lead you to a house. Explain to the owner that we need a room to eat the Passover Feast. He will show you to a large upstairs room. Get everything ready there.'

They followed his instructions, and in the evening Jesus arrived with the rest of the disciples.

The Passover Feast took on a new meaning that night. Jesus was preparing himself and his followers for his death.

He broke the bread and handed it round. 'This is my body,' he said. Then he passed round a cup of wine and said, 'This is my blood. When you eat the bread and drink the wine, remember me.'

We call this the Lord's Supper. Followers of Jesus all over the world, remember him in this way, still.

Jesus and his friends then sang a Psalm of praise together, before they went outside.

Jesus and his disciples went to a garden called Gethsemane.

'Sit here,' he said, 'while I go over there to pray.'

He took Peter and James and John with him. 'I am troubled,' he said. 'Stay here and keep me company.'

He went a little further on and fell down on his face and prayed to God his Father.

When he came back to the disciples, he found them sleeping. All the worry had exhausted them.

'Why are you sleeping?' Jesus asked. 'Get up and pray.'

While he was still speaking, Judas Iscariot and a crowd of men approached him. He came up to greet Jesus with a kiss. But Judas had made an agreement with Jesus' enemies. They had given him money to hand Jesus over to them.

When the disciples saw what was happening they wanted to fight. One of them lashed out with his sword and cut off the ear of the high priest's servant. But Jesus said, 'No more of this!' He touched the man's ear and it was healed immediately.

The crowd of men arrested Jesus and led him away to the high priest's house.

Peter followed the crowd at a distance. While Jesus was being questioned and bullied in the high priest's house, Peter stayed in the courtyard. He sat down by the fire. A servant girl peered at him. 'This man was with Jesus,' she said.

'I don't know him,' Peter exclaimed.

Later someone else said, 'You are one of them.'

'I am not,' said Peter hotly.

Then someone said, 'This man was with Jesus – he is a Galilean.'

'I don't know what you are talking about,' declared Peter.

Just then a cockerel crowed at daybreak. Jesus looked over to Peter and caught his eye. How ashamed Peter felt. He went out and wept bitterly. He had let Jesus down. He had denied him.

Jesus was sent then to Pilate the Roman Governor.

'Are you the King of the Jews?' Pilate asked.

'Yes, that is so,' replied Jesus.

'I do not find any fault with this man,' declared Pilate.

'But he is causing trouble in the whole country!' was the claim.

When Pilate heard that Jesus was from Galilee he packed him off to Herod. Herod was pleased to see Jesus at last and asked him many questions. But Jesus was silent.

Herod and the soldiers cruelly mocked him and dressed him up in a purple robe, and then sent him back to Pilate.

Pilate could still find no fault. 'I have the power to release one prisioner during this Feast week. I could release Jesus,' he suggested.

'No!' shouted the crowd. 'We do not want you to release Jesus. We want you to release Barabbas the robber.

Pilate appealed to them once again. But the crowd shouted out again, 'Crucify him! Crucify him!'

Jesus was led away to be crucified. This was a cruel death – being nailed to a wooden cross.

Jesus was forced to carry the big wooden cross on his back at first but then they allowed him to get help from a man called Simon.

Crowds of people followed him. Many of the women were crying loudly.

When they reached the place called Golgotha, they nailed Jesus to the cross and lifted it up.

Jesus was not angry. He prayed to God saying, 'Father forgive them, for they do not realise what they are doing.'

What love he showed, even at that time.

Jesus saw John standing nearby and asked him to look after Mary as if she were his own mother. John took Mary to live in his home from that day on.

Two thieves were crucified along with Jesus. One of them knew he deserved his punishment and realised that Jesus was the Son of God. 'Remember me when you come to your kingdom,' he asked.

Jesus promised, 'Today you will be with me in Paradise.'

In the final moments of his life, the thief asked Jesus for mercy. Jesus showed him love by forgiving his sin.

From twelve noon until three o'clock in the afternoon there was darkness over the whole land. How frightening! Jesus was bearing the full punishment for all the sins of his people.

'Why have you left me alone?' he called out to God his Father in agony.

Just before he died he shouted out with a loud voice, 'Father into your hands I commit my spirit.'

The big curtain in the temple was torn in two from the top to the bottom. Then the earth quaked and the rocks were split open. These miraculous things amazed the soldiers and others standing by. 'This was certainly the Son of God,' they declared.

That evening a rich man called Joseph went boldly to Pilate and asked permission to bury Jesus' body.

Joseph and his friend Nicodemus carefully took Jesus' body from the cross, wrapped him in a linen cloth and placed his body in a tomb in a garden. This was a large cave cut out of the rock.

A big stone was placed at the mouth of the cave like a door. The big stone was sealed and a guard was set to keep watch.

How sad Jesus' friends must have felt that Sabbath day. Jesus was dead. What would happen next?

Early in the morning of the first day of the week (we call it Sunday), some ladies came to the tomb. They wanted to prepare Jesus' body with spices. They were concerned about the big stone at the door of the tomb. Who would roll it away for them?

When they reached the tomb, what a surprise they got. The stone was rolled away already and an angel was sitting on it. One of the ladies ran to tell Peter and John what had happened. The others looked inside the tomb and found two angels.

'Do not be afraid,' one said. 'I know you are looking for Jesus. Do not look for him here. He is risen from the dead.'

The first person to see the risen Lord Jesus was Mary Magdalene. She was weeping in the garden, because she did not know what had happened to Jesus. She spoke to a man she thought was the gardener. The man spoke her name, 'Mary!' and she immediately realised that he was Jesus.

Mary ran with the good news to the disciples.

In the days that followed, Jesus appeared to all the disciples and to many other people too. Over five hundred people saw Jesus, risen from the dead.

He came right into the room where the disciples were hiding. They were terrified but he said to them, 'Peace be with you.'

Cleopas and his friend were walking along the road to Emmaus, talking about all that had happened in Jerusalem during the past few days.

Jesus came along beside them and walked with them but they thought he was a stranger. They were upset at how events had turned out. The man explained from the Old Testament all that had happened to Jesus.

When they reached Emmaus they persuaded the man to come into the house for some food for it was late.

When they sat down for supper, Jesus took the bread, blessed it and handed them a piece. Just then they realised that he was the risen Lord Jesus.

He disappeared from their sight. They then understood all that had been said on the road.

They rushed back to Jerusalem to tell the disciples. 'The Lord really has risen,' they said.

Sometime later seven of the disciples went fishing on the sea of Galilee. They fished all night but caught nothing. As they came back to the beach, they noticed a man standing there. This was in fact Jesus, but they didn't know that. 'Have you anything to eat?' the man asked.

'No!' they replied.

'Put your net down again,' he said. When they did that, they caught a huge number of fish.

John then recognised Jesus. 'It's the Lord,' he said
to Peter. Peter jumped into the sea to rush ashore
ahead of the boat. On the shore, Jesus had a fire
ready and had cooked some fish and bread. They
had a lovely breakfast together.

Jesus and his disciples went out of the city to the Mount of Olives. Jesus told his disciples that they would be his witnesses at home and in many places, telling others the good news of the Gospel. He lifted up his hands to bless them and he was lifted up into heaven, right through the clouds. The disciples were astounded. They stood gazing up into the sky where Jesus had gone.

Two men in white clothes stood beside them.

'Why are you standing there staring? Just as you have seen Jesus being taken up into heaven, he will return to earth one day.'

This filled the disciples with joy. They went to work with new energy, praising God and preaching his word everywhere they went.

Followers of Jesus are still telling this wonderful story all over the world today. This is the most important event in history.

We can have new life if we trust that what he has done for us on the cross has paid the price for our sins.

This is the good news of the gospel. We must believe it and pass it on to others.